# Soap Box Derby Racing

☆ ☆ ☆ ☆ ☆

*The opening parade, 1979, in Akron, Ohio, where the All-American Soap Box Derby is run.*

# Soap Box Derby Racing

## Sylvia A. Rosenthal

Lothrop, Lee & Shepard Books ☆ New York

**PHOTO CREDITS**

*Burbank Kiwanis Club, page 13. Burbank Daily Review, pages 10, 16, 18, 19, 21. The Montrose Ledger, page 120. All other photographs are courtesy of All-American Soap Box Derby and Jeff Iula of the Derby staff.*

*First Edition*

*1  2  3  4  5  6  7  8  9  10*

*Library of Congress Cataloging in Publication Data*
Rosenthal, Sylvia A.
  Soap box derby racing.

  Includes index.
  SUMMARY: Relates the history of the All-American Soap Box Derby, including profiles of some of the winners and losers and descriptions of memorable moments.
    1. Soap box derbies—History—Juvenile literature.  [1. Soap box derbies—History]
I. Title.
GV1029.7.R63      796.6      79-26439
ISBN 0-688-41915-1     ISBN 0-688-51915-6 (lib. bdg.)

# Acknowledgments

Without the help of these people, this book would not have been written:

Nancy Abruzzo, children's librarian, Burbank [California] Public Library, who suggested that I write it;

Richard Kermode, who lent me his memorabilia and acted as my technical adviser;

Lois Atkinson, teacher extraordinaire, who gave me invaluable advice and encouragement.

I would also like to thank:

All-American Soap Box Derby, especially Mr. Wayne L. Alley, general manager

Akron *Beacon Journal*

Burbank *Daily Review*

Burbank Kiwanis Club

Dayton *Daily News*

General Motors

Montrose *Ledger*

Ohio Historical Society Library

Reference Department, Burbank Central Library

And a special thanks to Jeff Iula of the All-American Soap Box Derby staff, for his help with the photographs and permission to reproduce those from his private collection.

# Contents

*1979 Junior Division World Champion Russ Yurk*

# 1 ☆ The Making of a Champion

For days big banners had been hung overhead at several of the main intersections in Burbank, California:

**LOS ANGELES COUNTY SOAP BOX DERBY**
**OLIVE AVENUE AND GLENOAKS**
**JULY 8, 1978**

The Burbank *Daily Review*, co-sponsor of the event, had been running feature stories about the coming derby. The other co-sponsor, the Burbank Kiwanis Club, had supplied manpower, as well as financial help. Surety Savings and Loan Association, whose building faced Olive Avenue, helped with a flashing sign reminding passersby: "Soap Box Derby in Burbank Saturday."

At last it was the morning of July 8, and preparations were under way to start the race. Olive Avenue, in downtown Burbank, had been roped off and converted into a temporary racetrack. It had a good slope and had been recently resurfaced. Bales of hay had been placed at strategic places as a safety factor.

It was a warm day, with the temperature hovering in the high eighties. The spectators—parents and friends of the contestants, firemen from the adjoining fire station, policemen assigned to duty, Burbank residents of all ages—stood on the adjoining sidewalks to watch the race. Some people had shown enough foresight to bring folding chairs and beach umbrellas. Children were sitting along the curb.

There were forty contestants, including Gayle Kermode, thirteen, of Glendale, California, one of five girls entered

*The pit, on Olive Avenue in Burbank, where the inspection and weighing of racers took place for the 1978 Los Angeles County Soap Box Derby.*

in the race. She and the other drivers, along with the derby officials, were crowded into a makeshift pit. This was a roped-off section in the middle of the street where the officials made a final inspection of the cars, checking to make sure they met derby regulations and safety rules. The officials also weighed the racers, with their drivers seated in them, to see that they didn't exceed the maximum limit.

There were two classifications of drivers: Junior Division and Senior Division. Prior to 1976, thirteen- to fifteen-year-olds were placed in Group A, and eleven- and twelve-year-olds were in Group B. After racing the members of their own groups, the winners of Group A and Group B raced each other to determine who would represent the local derby in the All-American finals in Akron, Ohio.

In 1976 boys and girls ten through twelve were given a class of their own, Junior Division, to race in. Now, ten-year-olds could race, and eleven- and twelve-year-olds had a fairer chance of winning when they didn't have to compete against the older contestants.

The combined weight of car and driver for the Junior Division could not be more than 220 pounds. For Senior Division drivers, ages twelve through fifteen, the combined weight could not exceed 250 pounds. (Twelve-year-olds had the option of racing in either the Junior or the Senior Division.)

While they were waiting for the race to begin, the contestants made last-minute inspections of their cars or gave them another rubdown. Some chatted with parents or friends. Others ate snacks or gulped down cold drinks. A few popped bubblegum. One Junior Division boy relieved his nervousness by going over to the curb and throwing up.

A reporter, spotting Gayle, went over to interview her. "When did you start racing?" she asked.

"Two years ago in Orange County," answered Gayle. "I was lucky. I placed third in the Junior Division."

The reporter smiled at the slim, auburn-haired girl, who seemed to have so much poise for her age. Gayle pushed some long strands of hair out of her eyes and smiled back.

"Are you scared when you're racing?"

"I was at first," Gayle replied, "especially when I crashed. I've been in seven crashes. But I don't mind the crashes any more. They're kind of fun."

"Fun?" the reporter asked in a startled voice.

"Sure," said Gayle. "When you hit something and start swinging around in circles, it's like being on one of those amusement park rides."

"Have you won many races?"

Gayle's brother Brian, sixteen, who was standing nearby, interjected, "She's got a whole shelfful of trophies."

"Have you and your brother ever raced against each other?"

Brian smiled. "Do you want to tell her what happened at Acton [California], Gayle?"

"Oh, yeah. Before our race started, Brian and I wanted to take a trial run to see whose car was faster. We set our cars on the ramp and got in. We rolled off the ramp like two bullets.

*Gayle Kermode and her father in their garage-workshop, preparing for the 1978 Los Angeles County Soap Box Derby. Gayle is in a reclining position to drive her lay-back racer. She is reaching forward inside the car to grasp the steering wheel. Her father is holding the cockpit cover, which folds down over the cockpit. During the race, all one can see of the driver is the top of her helmet and her eyes.*

"I'm always nervous on my first run because I don't know the hill. Everything was going wrong. The hill was so bumpy I couldn't see anything. Both Brian and I were swerving all over the track."

"When we passed the finish line," said Brian, "I put on my brake. The car hit a pothole and wham! I ran into Gayle's car and wrecked it."

"I did the same to your car, too, Brian. Don't you remember?"

"Oh, sure. And Dad helped us fix the cars so we still got to race."

"What I can't understand," said Gayle, "was how I managed to win a first-place trophy when my car's axles were still bent every which way!"

"But who won the race between you and Brian?" asked the reporter.

"Oh, it was a tie," laughed Gayle.

"What has been your most exciting race so far, Gayle?"

"The National Derby Rally in Warren, Ohio, in 1977. There were cars there from twenty-five states and Canada. Eighty-five cars were entered in the Junior Division. I came in third."

"How long did it take you to build your racer?"

"About two hundred hours. Actually, I had to build it *two* times. What a surprise it was when I went to take my first trial run and found out I couldn't get into my racer because I had gotten bigger around the hips!"

"Part of the price you had to pay for being a 'growing girl,' " said the reporter sympathetically.

"Yes. And the worst part was that I measured the new racer wrong. At the first inspection at my Derby Clinic, they told me I had to cut an inch off the nose!"

"Well, it looks beautiful now, Gayle. What does this race today mean to you?"

"If I come in first, I get to compete in the All-American Soap Box Derby in Akron, Ohio, for the championship of the world."

The interview was cut short by an announcement over the public address system. The derby was about to begin. "Oh, excuse me. I've got to go now," said Gayle as she rushed off.

The derby opened with a small parade led down the three-block hill by the color guard of the local Boy Scout troop, followed by the Burbank Junior Police Band. Right behind them was a Model T Ford, in which rode former Los Angeles County derby winners Curt Williamson and Anthony Wheeler. Bringing up the rear marched the soap box derby contestants, Gayle among them. When the parade dispersed at the foot of the hill, the contestants ran back up the sidewalk to the racing pit.

After the playing of "The Star-Spangled Banner," the Reverend Larry Stamper stepped up to the sidewalk microphone to give the invocation. Councilman Vern Gibson brought greetings from the City of Burbank. Then there were a few words of welcome from Dr. James Lark, representing the Kiwanis Club, and Irving Shear, Burbank *Daily Review* editor.

This was to be a photo swap race, which, since its intro-

*The contestants parade down Olive Avenue before the derby begins.*

duction in Southern California in 1976, has spread to many other localities. In a single-heat race, a camera takes a picture of the finish and a winner is announced. In a photo swap race, the winner is not declared until the two racers have raced *two* times against each other.

After the first race, the finish is photographed and the difference between the noses of the cars is measured. The cars then exchange wheels, which are provided by the Derby Association, and also exchange lanes. They race a second time, and again the difference between the cars at the finish is photographed and measured. The distances for the two races are totaled, and the racer with the highest winning margin wins the heat. The winner is eligible to race in another heat. The loser is eliminated from the race.*

Since it takes two runs to make one heat, each car has had a chance to race in both lanes and on both sets of wheels. Because lanes and wheels can get out of calibration, many derby enthusiasts think the photo swap way of racing is fairer. The drawback, of course, is that it takes twice as long as the single-heat race.

At 9 A.M. the first two Junior Division racers were rolled onto the starting ramp and the race began. The children sitting along the curb jumped up in excitement and pressed against the ropes. "Get back! You'll get hit!" they were cautioned. Reluctantly, they sat down again.

This heat was followed by one between two Senior Division racers; throughout the day, Junior and Senior Division cars ran in alternate heats. In round 1 the crowd let out a cry as one of the contestants lost control of his car, after crossing the finish line, and smashed into the curb. The race was held up as an ambulance, siren screeching, rushed to the scene and paramedics attended to the unlucky boy.

There was further delay because of difficulty with the camera. Finally, Gayle Kermode's first heat was called. On her first run down the hill, she trailed by a car length.

---

* The number of heats depends on the number of contestants. After each heat is run, the loser is eliminated. When there are only two winners left, these two race in a final heat for first place.

*Archie Melendrez of Cerritos (left) and Brenda Ohl of Simi Valley leaving the starting gate during one of the elimination heats.*

There was consternation among the Kermodes. Was this a bad omen?

Gayle's father tried to encourage her before the second half of the heat. "Remember, Gayle, just drive straight."

Gayle and her opponent switched wheels and lanes. After their cars had been placed on the ramp, the boy she was racing discovered that he had a brake problem. After five minutes spent working on the brakes without success, he withdrew from the heat and Gayle was declared automatic winner of that heat.

Heat after heat was run as the day wore on. Outwardly, at least, Gayle looked calm, but she refused to eat or drink anything the entire day. Her anxious mother coaxed her, but she kept saying, "I don't want to lose my turn when I'm called. I want to be ready to go."

Since there were forty contestants and each one got two chances to race in each heat, Gayle had a long time to wait for her turn. She had been at the racetrack for twelve hours now and had raced in six heats. She was numb with fatigue.

Finally, everybody in the Senior Division had been eliminated but Gayle Kermode and Linda Olsen. It was a threatening situation for Gayle. For some reason, Linda's yellow racer had been getting faster, and Gayle's burgundy-colored racer was slowing down.

Linda had beaten Gayle by an overall margin of 54 inches in one heat, whereas Gayle had defeated her in

*A car length ahead of the other racers, a driver heads toward the finish line.*

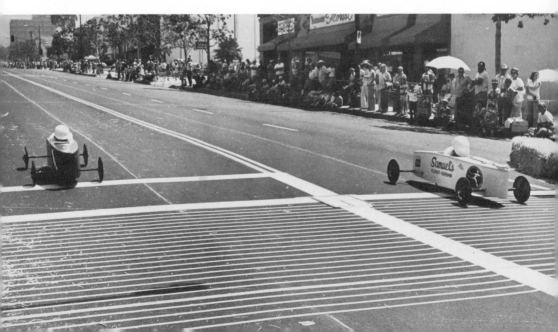

another heat by only 23 inches. This gave each girl one loss in the double elimination race. The next heat was the final one. It would determine who was going to represent Los Angeles in the nationals at the All-American in Akron.

The Kermodes were desperate. Something had to be done to Gayle's racer if she were to win! Derby officials permitted each contestant to check the alignment and make minor adjustments to their racers prior to the final heat. Gayle's pit crew—her father and brother—looked at the alignment. It was perfect. The kingpin nut looked a little loose, though, so they tightened it.

Gayle and Linda put new wheels on their racers. The tension mounted as the girls got ready to take off. It was now 8:30 P.M., and so dark that it was difficult to see. Gayle sighted the nose of her racer on the headlights of passing cars on the street below the racecourse.

The little racers whizzed down the track. Gayle nosed out Linda by 13 inches. But how would she do when they changed lanes? Would she have enough of a margin to overcome any lead Linda might gain in the second half of the heat? The girls swapped wheels and lanes. This would be Gayle's thirteenth run down the hill!

Gayle was nervous as she slid into her "lay-back" racer for the final heat. Her brother Brian stuck his head inside the car and made a face. This made her laugh and relieved some of her tension. She drove a perfect race.

The ending of the race was a really close one. Linda Olsen was first declared the winner by 12 inches. But thirteen turned out to be Gayle's lucky number, for the announcer soon boomed out a correction. Since Gayle had won the first half of the heat by 13 inches, she had an overall winning margin of *one inch*. Gayle Kermode was declared the winner of the Senior Division race and became

*Gayle Kermode of Glendale, Senior Division, and John Van Dyke of Sun Valley, Junior Division, won an expense-paid trip to the All-American Soap Box Derby in Akron, Ohio, to compete in the nationals.*

the first girl champion in the history of the Los Angeles County Soap Box Derby.

There were loud cheers from the spectators, and, as her mother hugged her, Gayle burst into tears. For Gayle's father, Richard Kermode, her win had special significance. He himself had raced in 1941. His brother, Howard Kermode, had been Los Angeles champion in 1949. And his son Brian, Gayle's brother, had been runner-up twice in the local derby races, losing both times by only one inch—just the margin that Gayle had won by.

As first-place winner, Gayle won a $100 savings bond and $1,000 for expenses to go to Akron to compete in the 41st running of the All-American Soap Box Derby!

# 2 ☆ From Downhill Fun to Gravity Grand Prix

It was many years ago, and 2,180 miles from Burbank, that soap box racing became an organized sport. In the summer of 1933 three young boys, just for fun, were racing soap box cars down a steep brick street in Dayton, Ohio. A slope was needed for racing, as these motorless cars were propelled only by the force of gravity.

Myron E. Scott, photographer for the Dayton *Daily News*, happened to be passing by. He was looking for material to fill his picture column in the *Daily News*, so he snapped some photographs of the racing boys. This gave him an idea for a newspaper story. He asked the boys if they would like to have a real race, with prizes for the winners. They agreed it would be fun and volunteered to spread the word among their friends.

The following Saturday, several dozen boys showed up for the race. The boys' cars varied in size, shape, and style. Some were made from boxes that had contained soap. Some used peach crates and bread boxes for hoods, roller skates for wheels, and any other kind of material the boys could scrounge. One boy had mounted a pair of axles and wheels from an old baby carriage on a two-by-six plank and had stuck a soap box in front.

Hundreds of spectators crowded the street, causing a traffic tie-up. Myron Scott snapped pictures and handed out the prizes. His newspaper story, with its action photographs, made a tremendous hit with the readers. Scott suggested to his editor that the *Daily News* sponsor a city-wide race.

Scott thought up the name "soap box derby," and on Saturday August 19, 1933, the first soap box derby in the United States was held. There was a big parade through downtown Dayton. Participating were the Firemen's Band, the American Legion Drum Corps, the Boy Scout Band, and numerous floats. Seated in their racers, 362 drivers were towed down the street by automobiles.

The racers were inspected and put into four divisions: Class A, for plain-bearing wheels; Class B, for roller-bearing or ball-bearing wheels; Class C, for cars with pneumatic tires; and Class D, for all specially built cars. There were two age groups, one for boys under eleven and another for boys eleven to sixteen. Seventy-five prizes were to be awarded.

The race was to be run on the well-used Burkhardt coasting hill. The surrounding bluffs made this an ideal viewing place for the spectators, and 40,000 people lined the track. Boy Scouts had set up a first-aid tent, but fortunately there were few accidents.

A maximum of five cars were allowed to participate in each heat, followed by the elimination races. Vehicles of all kinds competed. Some were crudely made; others were beautifully constructed. Occasionally, a poorly made car collapsed. The first heat was run at 2 P.M.; the last, at 5:30 P.M. David Wyse, ten, won a bicycle for boys eleven years and under. Randall Custer, sixteen, in a flashing yellow comet, won the *Daily News* trophy for boys over eleven.

There was one girl in the race: Alice Johnson, eleven, daughter of a well-known local aviator, Al Johnson. She had lost to Randall Custer. When Custer was given a bouquet of flowers, he walked over and gave them to Alice. The crowd let out a roar of approval.

The three major newsreel companies filmed the event. The newsreels were shown in theaters throughout the country. Many youngsters and their families, learning about soap box racing, became interested in organizing races in their own communities.

Chevrolet agreed to become co-sponsor with the Dayton *Daily News* for the 1934 derby. Chevrolet dealers throughout the country became sponsors to local groups in staging races. The winners of these races were to go to Dayton for the nationals.

In August 1934, the soap box derby was run for the first time under its new name: The All-American Soap Box Derby. Thirty-four cities sent contestants to Dayton, so it had to be made into a two-day event. The Dayton

and All-Ohio Soap Box Derby races were to be run on the first day and the nationals on the second day.

Owners of land along the racetrack had given permission to put up stands, so there were seats for 30,000 people. There was room for thousands more to stand and watch along the paved track, three eighths of a mile long. The track had a 15 percent grade, sloping down to 6 percent, and ending in a level straightaway.

A bridge had been built at the finish line. The judges and other officials communicated from there with people at the starting line. All the races were timed. Results of the races were carried by loudspeakers that had been placed along the racecourse.

As it had the year before, the derby opened with a parade. This was to become a yearly tradition. On August 18, the day of the local races, Alice Johnson was joined by a second girl, Evelyn Beddies. It would be many years before another girl would race in the soap box derby.

The favorite of the crowd was Jack Colopy, thirteen, who had beaten four hundred other Dayton racers. His was a real soap box creation—it was so simply built from parts he had found in a junkyard that it had cost him only fifty-five

*Alice Johnson, only girl driver in the 1933 soap box race, is surrounded by the other winners in the photo at top left. She is holding flowers given her by Randall Custer (top right), who came in first. Myron E. Scott, "father" of the soap box derby, is shown in photo number 3. Photo number 4 shows Bob Gravett of Oakwood, Ohio, in the car he drove in the Blue Flame race. Photos 5 and 6 show part of a heat.*

cents. His boosters groaned when he lost the All-Ohio by half a length.

On Sunday August 19, the winner of the All-Ohio met the champions from the other states in the All-American race. As an added attraction, the day's events were concluded with another race, the "Blue Flame." This was for specially built speedy racing cars driven by sixteen- to eighteen-year-olds.

The prizes were generous—over one hundred of them, given by different stores. First prize was a four-year college scholarship. Second prize was a three-day expense-paid trip to the World's Fair, which was being held in Chicago that year.

On Sunday afternoon, before the start of the All-American, NBC's outstanding radio announcer Graham McNamee rode down the hill in a soap box racer, describing the track as he went along. Newsreel cameramen photographed the races.

The three finalists in the race were started off by Colonel Roscoe Turner, the cross-country flyer who had set many records. The winner of the first All-American Soap Box Derby was Robert Turner, eleven, of Muncie, Indiana, whose winning time was 58.4 seconds. The newspapers wrote about the coincidence of two Turners—no relation, but both speed demons. Since that time, Bob Turner has remained active in derby racing and has never missed

*The first All-American Soap Box Derby was held in Dayton, Ohio, in 1934. Photo number 1 shows the winner, Robert Turner of Muncie, Indiana (photo number 2), crossing the finish line. A large crowd watched the race (photo number 3). Graham McNamee, NBC's outstanding radio announcer, is shown in photo number 4. Before the start of the All-American, he rode down the track in a soap box racer, broadcasting on a nationwide radio hook-up as he went along. Jack Furstenberg of Omaha, Nebraska, won the E. V. Rickenbacker trophy for the fastest heat and the Charles F. Kettering cup for the best-constructed racer (photo number 5).*

*Robert Turner is shown here receiving a $500 insurance policy from Myron Scott, founder of the soap box derby.*

attending the All-American Soap Box Derby. He is as well known in Akron as any movie star.

It was decided to move the All-American to Akron in 1935 because of Akron's central location and hilly terrain, and because Akron officials promised a permanent race-track. The race was first run on a city street, Tallmadge Hill. There were fifty-two contestants and twenty thousand spectators. The winner was Maurice E. Bale, Jr., fourteen, of Anderson, Indiana.

Bale's winning was overshadowed by an even more newsworthy story: the accident that sent Graham McNamee and his fellow radio announcer, Tom Manning, to the hospital. They had stepped beyond the barrier fences, near the finish line, to watch the race, though they were warned that it was against the rules and dangerous. McNamee minimized the danger, saying, "I've broadcast from a plane high in the sky, from a submarine on the ocean bottom, from the fastest cars at Indianapolis. I'm not afraid of a little thing like a kiddiecar!"

Shortly after he made this remark, the finalists came racing down the hill: Paul Brown of Oklahoma City, Loney Kline of Akron, and Maurice Bale, the eventual winner. Three fourths of the way down the track, Brown's tire tape came off, causing his car to swerve off course and crash

*The All-American Soap Box Derby moved to Akron in 1935, and Maurice Bale of Anderson, Indiana, was the winner that year.*

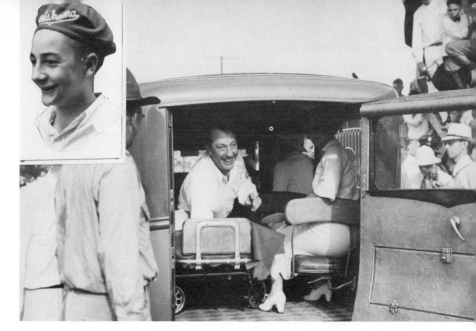

Graham McNamee, NBC radio announcer, smiling from the ambulance taking him to the hospital after he was hit by a soap box racer driven by Paul Brown of Oklahoma City, shown above left.

The All-American went international in 1936 with an entrant from South Africa. Herbert Muench, Jr., of St. Louis, shown in the winner's circle being interviewed, upheld the honor of the Americans by beating him.

into McNamee and Manning. Newspapers all over the United States and the world featured the accident and people asked, "What is a Soap Box Derby?" The next year the number of entrants increased from 52 to 117!

Two important events happened to the All-American in 1936. It became an international event with an entrant from South Africa; however, Herbert Muench, Jr., fourteen, of St. Louis, Missouri, upheld the honor of the Americans by defeating the South African entrant. And, for the first time, the derby was taken off the streets and run on its own racetrack. It had now acquired some of the same kind of prestige as its adult counterpart, the Indianapolis 500, and could call itself "The World's Gravity Grand Prix."

*In 1936 the All-American Soap Box Derby was taken off the street when it acquired its own track in Akron. Looking at the newly built track are the Derby's founding fathers: (left to right) Jim Schlemmer, Myron Scott, Jack Gormley, Shorty Fulton.*

# 3 ☆ Crashes, Mishaps, and Other Handicaps

It takes courage to be the driver of a soap box racer. The driver of even a small automobile has about 2,000 pounds of steel and other materials as protection. A boy or girl driving a soap box racer has less than 250 pounds, including his or her own weight.

Soap box racers have not been built in a factory by trained mechanics, but by their drivers (with limited help from advisers), using simple materials and comparatively simple tools. Even with the finest craftsmanship, it is possible that something can break as the car vibrates on the racetrack. If a brake fails, there is no motor to help stop the car, which may be going as fast as 35 m.p.h.!

Fortunately, there have been no fatalities in the All-American Soap Box Derby, though it has had its share of crashes and near-misses. (The All-American insists that all entrants wear crash helmets and pass rigid safety requirements.) In the very first All-American Soap Box Derby, in 1934, there were two accidents. About two thirds of the way down the hill, Alice Johnson's car started weaving wildly from side to side. The crowd screamed with fright, but she managed to regain control and rode on to win the heat. Bobbie Turner, after racing his car to a first-place finish, sped 150 yards past the end line and crashed into the side of the track. His car was ruined, but he emerged smiling and unhurt.

*World champion in 1939, Cliff Hardesty of White Plains, New York, is congratulated by E. M. Coyle, General Motors representative.*

In 1939 Clifton Hardesty of White Plains, New York, was subjected to a barrage of pressures. Some people didn't think that an eleven-year-old boy could have built such a beautifully constructed racer, so the Derby officials bombarded him with questions. As a final test, they took him to an Akron trade school, where he handled tools like a real pro and practically built a racer before their eyes! He had another ordeal when he took his car on a trial run and had the bad luck to crack up. However, he made a quick recovery and after the car was repaired went on to win first place.

Another crack-up victim was Gilbert Klecan of San Diego, California, winner of the 1946 Derby. Averaging 35 m.p.h. down the track, he crossed the finish line, crashed into the film truck, and broke two ribs. He mended fast and shortly thereafter got a part in the movie *Magic Town*, starring Jimmy Stewart, who had been one of the entertainers at the Derby.

The 13th All-American Soap Box Derby in 1950 proved to be a lucky one for Harold Williamson, a contestant from Charleston, West Virginia, whose physical activity was limited because he had been a victim of rheumatic fever from age nine. Since he had had to forego other sports, he put all his energy into building a soap box racer. His efforts paid off with a first-place win.

In the 1951 Derby, Jack Wyatt of Anderson, Indiana, had a close call. He was only a few feet from the finish line when a dog trotted out onto the track. He couldn't avoid hitting the dog, and the car skidded and ran into the side boards. The car was damaged slightly, but Jack wasn't injured and evidently the dog wasn't either, as he ran off.

The following year, 1952, Columbus, Georgia, contestant Joe Lunn cracked up in his first heat. While he was in the first-aid tent getting patched up, his car was being patched up by the mechanics. The repairs were so evident that the racer was nicknamed "The Rambling Wreck from Georgia Tech." Joe went on to race four more heats, winning the final one in 27.77 seconds.

The spectators felt great sympathy for a non-winner in the 1955 race, Los Angeles entrant Lynn Erickson. It had been well publicized that he had spent an unusual amount of time (500 hours) working on his car, so it was a real heartbreaker when his brakes broke. Lynn thought the

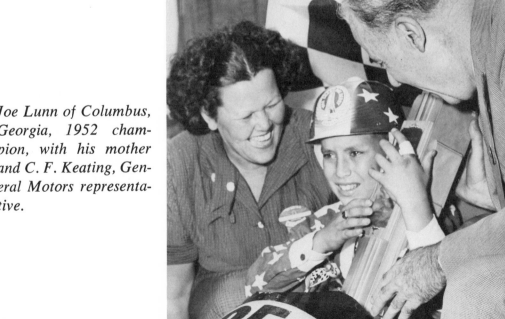

*Joe Lunn of Columbus, Georgia, 1952 champion, with his mother and C. F. Keating, General Motors representative.*

delay to repair his car would be too lengthy; not wanting to hold up the race, he forfeited his place. For this gesture he received the good sportsmanship award.

Norman Westfall of Rochester, New York, also had some bad luck. His racer was damaged in being shipped to the Derby and had to be repaired. Then at weigh-in he was two and a half pounds over the limit, so more alterations had to be done to the car. Despite this bad start, Norman went on to win the 1956 Derby.

The 1959 winner, Barney Townsend of Anderson, Indiana, was put in a somewhat precarious position by having broken his collarbone previous to the race. The doctor removed his cast before he left for Akron, but advised him to be *very* careful. Barney gingerly inched his body into the racer and, fortunately, avoided further injury during the race.

Two 1964 contestants drove with broken arms. Larry Thienes, eleven, of Indianapolis fell out of a tree and broke his arm two weeks before the Derby was to begin. Because he had to have a cast put on his arm, the top edge of his racer's cockpit had to be cut away to give him extra room. Freddy Trost, fifteen, of Plattsburgh, New York, wore a cast-like bandage on his left arm, which he had broken falling from a horse. His doctor told him he could take off the bandage when he drove, as he didn't have time to modify his cockpit before the Derby began.

Rick Brown, 1966 contestant from Cedar Rapids, had the bad luck to fall out of his upper bunk at Derbytown, fracturing his shoulder. He was worried, not about his shoulder, but about missing the chance to race. Fortunately, the doctor gave him permission to drive his racer.

There were also broken bones among the 1967 contestants. Because of a broken foot, Mark Zoller of Cleveland had to hobble around on crutches. He used the crutches to hop in and out of his car! His cast, however, proved to be a handicap as it added four pounds excess weight to his car, necessitating some minor adjustments. Ed Ronsani broke his arm at his Hudson, New York, home playing "Walk the Barrel," so had to drive his racer with a cast on his arm from above the elbow down to the first knuckle.

A different kind of "handicap" was overcome in the 1970 Derby. The general rule in the Soap Box Derby is that "the builders of the racers must drive the racers they build. If some emergency recognized by the Derby Committee prevents you from racing, you may name a substitute driver for your car." The Derby Committee recognized Mark Christensen's "emergency." Mark, who was from Santa Cruz, California, couldn't race for religious reasons because race day was also his Sabbath. Another boy was permitted to drive his racer, and it placed third in the first heat.

That same year Matt Davis of Zanesville, Ohio, had a serious accident in heat 39 and was rushed to the hospital. After his broken left leg was set, he returned to watch the finals. The crowd gave him a standing ovation.

In 1976, for the first time in the Derby's history, all three cars racing in the same heat were involved in a crash. Senior Division driver Rory Busby lost control of his car and veered into the next lane, hitting the car driven by Robert Bullard. Both cars then struck the car driven by Mike Needs. Rory Busby was disqualified for crossing out of his lane. Mike and Robert raced again after their cars were repaired. Robert won.

In the Junior Division that year, John Underwood, eleven, the Akron champ, didn't feel very well during Derby week. He didn't complain about his pains because he didn't want to miss the race. Two days after the Derby he was rushed to the hospital, where he had his appendix removed.

Another courageous contestant was Lori Roth, who was pluckily winning her battle with cancer when she entered the 1978 Derby. All she was hoping for was to win just one heat. Lori got her wish, winning in the first round.

No doubt there will continue to be thrills, spills, and other misfortunes for the young contestants who enter the Soap Box Derby. But they seem to be a special breed of youngster, with the maturity to devote countless hours of spare time laboring over the construction of a soap box racer. Their adventuresome spirit enables them to accept the risks involved in this exciting sport for the thrill they receive in going down that hill.

# 4 ☆ Good-Luck Charms and Other Superstitions

The experts may scoff at them for being superstitious and non-scientific, but boys and girls who have driven soap box racers have had their own theories about what makes a winner. In one local race, a boy nailed a horseshoe from a famous race horse to the back of his car. Another boy shaved off all the hair from his head, thinking this would help combat the resistance of the wind. And in 1938 Bob Berger raced without his shirt and greased his back, also to cut down wind resistance. Derby officials thought this was a dangerous practice and inserted a clause in the rule book that shirts had to be worn.

A doctor once gave a young friend a stethoscope to carry for good luck. However, the young man found what he thought was a more practical use for it. He placed the stethoscope against the wheels of his car and listened to them before and after the race. "That's the only way I can tell if the bearings are in good working order," he said.

Then there was safety-conscious Gerald Long of Ann Arbor, Michigan, who put a bandage on his nose and forehead. He said, "I don't want to hurt myself if my head bangs onto the front of my racer."

One year the race was held up until a boy found his jeweler's rouge to rub into the moving parts of his car. The 1939 race was delayed for a different reason. A contestant wasn't happy until he was given some dry ice to put on his rubber tires "to cool them."

Because the weight can't be more than 250 pounds for the car and its driver, some contestants have had to use ingenuity when they were over the limit. Once a car from Alaska absorbed several pounds of moisture during its sea voyage. To get rid of its excess weight, the car was baked under lamps. One driver, discovering that *he* was overweight, sweated off the extra pounds by wrapping himself in blankets and sitting in front of a kerosene lamp for a couple of hours a day—in the heat of summer!

On the other hand, there was the boy who loaded himself up on bananas and water to put on weight. He tried to come as close as possible to the 250 pounds maximum because the heavier the car, the faster it goes down the hill.

The 1940 Derby winner, Tommy Fisher of Detroit, Michigan, raced in his stocking feet. And just before he started his last ride down the track, which led to his victory, he lost a tooth. He was so sure it was a lucky omen that when photographers snapped his picture, he purposely opened his mouth to show the gap where his tooth had been.

*Thomas Fisher of Detroit, 1940 world champion, with Wilbur Shaw, three-time Indianapolis Speedway winner.*

A boy in the 1946 Los Angeles race carried his pet duck as a passenger—"for good luck," he said. Others, however, suspected it was because the duck added fifteen pounds more weight to the racer!

The 1946 Derby winner, Gilbert Klecan of San Diego, California, rubbed graphite powder over both his racer and his face, again on the theory of cutting down on wind resistance. This act of his opened a "hornet's nest," as the following year many contestants followed his example. The cars were so slippery, the handlers kept dropping them! Graphite powder was soon added to the prohibited list in the rule book.

*Gilbert Klecan of San Diego, 1946 Derby winner, covered himself and his car with graphite on the theory that this would cut down on wind resistance.*

The 1947 contestants seem to have been an unusually interesting group. John Markey of White Plains, New York, tucked his trousers into his stockings to make himself more "streamlined." Don Meyer of Vallejo, California, put a piece of sponge rubber on the cockpit of his car, to rest his nose on before going down the track. Edward Hanson, of Columbus, Georgia, read from the Bible before he went down. Winner Kenneth Holmboe of Charleston, West Virginia, used a variety of good-luck charms. He raced in an old pair of shower slippers, carried a rabbit's foot, and wore a four-leaf clover.

There was also an unusually large number of good-luck pieces carried in the 1949 race. One racer had the baby shoes of its driver's nine-month-old sister tacked to the side of the cockpit. Other drivers carried pliers, religious medals, silver dollars, and a magnetic horseshoe. Winner Freddy Derks of Akron was more scientific. He tested several models in a wind tunnel before designing his racer, which he painted black "to absorb heat from the sun."

Some contestants have thought a certain name or number on their cars brought them good luck. Howard Kermode, 1949 Derby contestant from Los Angeles, named his racer "Stardust" after his favorite song, which he played on the trumpet in his high school band. Others chose a "lucky" number, seven being an especially popular one.

In 1951 winner Darwin Cooper of Williamsport, Pennsylvania, carried a good-luck charm bracelet belonging to his girl friend. A 1952 contestant, Roy Brooks, was afraid of biting his tongue, so he put a piece of sponge rubber between his teeth. The 1953 winner, Fred Mohler of Muncie, Indiana, carried his father's "lucky" gold piece.

*1953 champion Fred Mohler with his mother and father. Handing Fred his trophy is Robert Turner, 1934 champion. Both are from Muncie, Indiana.*

In the 1954 race, one boy's way of keeping down wind resistance was to put a rubber band around his chest to keep his shirt from blowing. Winner Dick Kemp of Los Angeles, however, had his own bag of tricks. He carefully lined up his wheels on the starting ramp a certain way, on the theory that each had a high spot. Then, for good measure, he carried a silver dollar that had been given to him by his Sunday school teacher.

Harold (Bo) Conrad of Duluth, Minnesota, 1963 winner, carried a good-luck piece that had great sentimental value to him. Tied to the webbing of his Derby helmet was the bronze hockey medal his late father had won. His father had died three years previous to the Derby, and Bo worked alone in his father's basement workshop, rebuilding the racer in which he had lost the 1962 local derby race.

The 1969 winner, Steve Souter of Midland, Texas, dusted off his wheels for good luck before getting into his racer. He also carried a note from Kenneth Cline, who was the winner in the 1967 Derby. Souter's was the first lay-back racer to win.

In 1970, Samuel Gupton of Durham, North Carolina, beat two hundred and fifty other contestants with his sleek black racer. He thought the black paint fought the wind resistance, enabling him to win, but his theory was disputed by others, who thought his victory was more likely due to the eight hundred hours he had worked on building the racer.

In 1976, the year that the United States celebrated its

In 1969 Steve Souter of Midland, Texas, drove the first lay-back racer to win the All-American.

bicentennial, Senior Division winner Joan Ferdinand of Canton, Ohio, appropriately wore a pewter Bicentennial medallion. The same medallion was worn in 1977 by her brother, Mark Ferdinand, when he won in the Junior Division. Senior Division winner that year, Steve Washburn of Bristol, Connecticut, carried a plastic drink stirrer shaped like a giraffe. But his *best* luck was in winning *two days* before his sixteenth birthday, which marked the end of his eligibility for the Soap Box Derby!

The 1978 Senior Division winner, Gregory Cardinal of Flint, Michigan, tied a green garter to his steering wheel. His brother, a 1977 contestant, had used it, but it hadn't brought him the luck it brought Greg. Los Angeles Derby contestant Gayle Kermode had never before carried anything for good luck until she was given a four-leaf clover to take to Akron by her local derby director, Cliff Wheeler. The four-leaf clover, which she taped inside her car, stayed with her to the finals.

The experts will probably continue to claim that it is a combination of a good car and a good driver that makes a winner. Nevertheless, the boys and girls who compete will probably go right on devising new gimmicks for winning. And, after all, how can the experts really prove that it *wasn't* Aunt Gussie's or Uncle Ike's good-luck charm, fastened to the racer's cockpit, that provided the margin of victory?

# 5 ☆ The Girls Join the Boys

Alice Johnson—what a girl she must have been! At a time when girls didn't engage in "rough" sports, this Dayton, Ohio, youngster had the courage to be the only girl racing in the first Soap Box Derby, in 1933. Not only that, she almost won it!

The spectators were making remarks about the "cute little guy" who had come in second as "he" went up to claim his prize. When he removed his cap, his long golden hair tumbled out. Gasps of surprise were heard as people said, "Why, it's a girl!"

What was her motivation? We can only guess. Was it her upbringing? Her father had been an intrepid aviator, and she might have inherited his adventuresome spirit. Adventuresome she was, all right, because she competed again in the 1934 Dayton derby. This time she finished third.

After that, she seems to have faded from Derby history. However, another Dayton girl, Evelyn Beddies, who was also in the local race, still makes news because of her interest in soap box derby racing. Now grown and married, Evelyn Beddies Hodgson says she was a tomboy when she

49

was eleven years old. Since the rules didn't specify the entrant had to be a boy, she entered the race. "Until they announced I was a girl, I don't think anyone knew," Mrs. Hodgson said. "I had a boy's haircut and wasn't very shapely at eleven."

Evelyn won her first three heats. After losing the fourth heat, she decided to go home for a drink and a short rest before returning, as she was hot and tired. She didn't know that the winner of that heat had accidentally driven off the track and wrecked his car.

"They called me on the loudspeaker, but I just didn't hear them because I was on the way home," Mrs. Hodgson recalls. "So they pulled my car out of the race."

She still wonders whether she might have won if she had stayed at the racetrack instead of going home. Perhaps one of her granddaughters, all of whom have raced in the Derby, will win for her someday! Her husband, son, and brother-in-law all help in soap box derby associations.

The rules must have been tightened after those early years, because girls were prohibited from racing. In 1947 a Los Angeles girl, June Kersey, tried to break into the local race. The judges said, "Sorry, no girls allowed!" She was so disappointed that they permitted her one trial run down the track.

It wasn't until 1971 that girls were officially permitted to race in the Soap Box Derby! Five girls participated in the All-American that year. Rebecca Phillips, eleven, of

Temple, Texas, won the opening heat and placed third in her second-round heat.

There were twenty-seven girls in the 1972 Derby. Two of them did quite well. Priscilla Freeman of Chapel Hill, North Carolina, placed fifth, and Karen Johnson of Motor City, Michigan, placed seventh.

In 1973 the girls did even better. Diane Mills of Putnam County, New York, won third place and a $4,000 college scholarship. Margaret Mary Zoller of Cleveland, Ohio, won sixth place and a $2,500 college scholarship. Diane's racer was called the "Pink Panther." Her family also "went pink," her mother wearing a pink dress and large pink hat and her father wearing a pink shirt. Diane must have been a steak lover because her father had promised her a steak for every heat she won! She was a favorite of the crowd, for they booed when the announcement was made, after her sixth run, that she had lost. This was hastily corrected a few minutes later when the picture of the photo finish showed that she had won.

The girls also made a respectable showing for themselves in the 1974 Derby. Of the twenty-one girls represented, eight won their first heats and three won their second heats. Kimberly Etchison of Anderson, Indiana, was so excited about winning fourth place that she kept jumping up and down, saying, "I can't believe it! I just can't believe it! I won! I won!"

The 1975 race was almost taken over by the girls. Twenty

of the one hundred contestants were girls, and they won five of the top nine places, including the Big One. They came out in this order:

| | |
|---|---|
| Karren L. Stead, 11, Lower Bucks County, Pa. | 1st |
| Kimberly Watts, 12, Charleston, W. Va. | 4th |
| Kathy Lewis, 12, Elk Grove, Calif. | 5th |
| Shelly Brower, 12, Newbury Park, Calif. | 6th |
| Kristine Oosting, 11, Grand Rapids, Mich. | 8th |

*Karren Stead of Lower Bucks County, Pennsylvania, in 1975 was the first girl to win the All-American. She didn't let a "little" thing like a dislocated thumb keep her from racing! The girls almost took over the 1975 Derby:*

*Kimberly Watts of Charleston, West Virginia, fourth-place winner;*

*Kathy Lewis of Elk Grove, California, fifth place;*

*Shelly Brower of Newbury Park, California, sixth place;*

*Kristy Oosting of Grand Rapids, Michigan, eighth place.*

Karren, 4'11" and 95 pounds when she raced, certainly had a lot of spunk. She drove wearing a cast extending from her hand to her elbow. (Just before the race, she had dislocated her thumb in a water-balloon fight with the other local champs at Derbytown.) She didn't let a "little" thing like a dislocated thumb keep her from racing!

The weather was bad, light rain falling during the first few heats. Attendance dropped to 10,000 people, but the spectators made up in enthusiasm what they lacked in numbers. As the racers came downhill in the winning heat, the noise level of the crowd built with the speed of the cars. In the 27.52 seconds from the start of the race to the finish line, thousands of people rose from their seats to view the photo-finish win.

The race the next year, 1976, was even more of a cliff-hanger. It had an unhappy beginning when, at the end of the second round, a heavy downpour held up activities for forty-five minutes, but an exciting finish more than made up for the delay. Joan Ferdinand, fourteen, of Canton, Ohio, had made four trips down the track. On her final run, a photograph of the finish showed her to be in a dead heat with John Pullium, fourteen, of Atlanta, Georgia, so there had to be a rerun. Again, the race was so close that the officials had to look at a photograph. Joan was finally declared the winner of the Senior Division, becoming the second girl to win the All-American.

When Karren Stead, 1975 winner, was asked how it felt to be the first female All-American Soap Box Derby champ,

*Joan Ferdinand of Canton, Ohio, who raced in the Senior Division in the 1976 Derby, was the second girl to win top honors in the All-American.*

she replied, "It doesn't make any difference whether you're a boy or a girl in a race like this."

Evidently it doesn't, because the San Francisco *Boys'* Club sent a girl, Rosalie Vierra, to represent them in the 1977 race! Another girl, Hope Barber, won third place in the Senior Division. Before coming to Akron, Hope had won her local race in the 40th running of the Dayton Derby, going down historical Burkhardt Hill where the very first Soap Box Derby had been run.

The 1978 Derby was held on a sweltering day, with the temperature soaring into the high nineties. Nevertheless, 9,500 spectators braved the heat to cheer for their favorites.

In the Junior Division, Jennifer Snyder of Conshohocken, Pennsylvania, placed second. Jennifer said she had had a funny experience in her local race. "I got the hiccups, so my car started going in and out. One of my friends said I looked like I was doing the Virginia Reel."

Deena Ferrin, who placed third, was superstitious. She wore the same clothes in the All-American that she had worn in winning her local race in Vallejo, California.

In the Senior Division, Laurie Sheetz of Lower Bucks

*Jennifer Snyder with the trophy she earned as 1978's second-place winner in the Junior Division.*

County, Pennsylvania, came in fifth. Laurie was glad there were no practical jokers at Derby Downs. Once when she was racing in a rally not connected with the Soap Box Derby, a boy sneakily put tape over the steering flaps of her car, which kept them closed. That was one heat Laurie didn't finish, as halfway down the hill, not having any steering, she had to brake to avoid hitting the car next to hers!

Gayle Kermode of Los Angeles, California, was sixth-place winner, and Joan Mabee of Mansfield, Ohio, won eighth place. Joan said, "When I grow up, I'd like to be in-

volved in the Derby as an organizer because the people that run these events are super, and they really care about the kids."

The exciting 1979 Derby not only drew 10,000 spectators, but a nationwide audience viewed it on TV when ABC broadcast it as part of their "Wide World of Sports" program.

Almost one fourth of the 1979 contestants were girls. Kim Van Pay of Green Bay, Wisconsin, tied Tony Clemente of Worcester, Massachusetts, for second place in the Junior Division. Lisa Schulz of Tidewater, Virginia, placed ninth. In the Senior Division, Prudence Short of Charleston, West Virginia, was fifth-place winner, and Kimberly Horseman of Augusta, Georgia, came in ninth.

Kim's family thought she was fated to win second place, she said, because "the number 2 kept popping up." Some examples she cited were:

Kim won the local race with number 102.
It was the 42nd All-American Soap Box Derby.
Kim was number 2 to sign in.
Her racing number was 132.
She drew heat 25 for her first race.
She raced in lane 2 *two* times.
There were 82 entrants in the Junior Division.

*Deena Ferrin stands by the trophy she won for third place and the racer that took her to victory.*

*These girls were winners in 1979: on this page, Kim Marie Van Pay, who tied for second place in the Junior Division; top right on opposite page, Lisa Schultz, ninth place in the Junior Division. In the Senior Division, Prudence Short, bottom, came in fifth, and Kim Horseman, top left, eighth.*

Whether fate should be credited with her win is doubtful. More likely, it was her enthusiasm that carried the day. As Kim put it, "There are a lot of people in Green Bay who live, eat, and sleep Derby!"

And the same could be said for girls all over the country. They have come a long way from 1933, when Alice Johnson was their lone representative!

# 6 ☆ Who Drives a Soap Box Racer?

America has been called a "melting pot"—meaning, of course, that it is made up of many different kinds of people. One might also call the Soap Box Derby a "melting pot." Soap box racer drivers come in all sizes, from very small to very large. They are athletes and non-athletes. They live in sparsely populated areas and big cities. And they include both girls and boys.

In soap box racing, unlike some other sports, stature and strength are not important, just as long as your body will fit inside a racer. The 1947 winner, Kenneth Holmboe of Charleston, West Virginia, barely managed to squeeze his long frame into his racing car. In the 1948 Derby, Jimmy Miller of Evansville, Indiana, had similar difficulty. He was wedged in his small cockpit so tightly that he had trouble getting out of his car at the finish line. The car handlers had to pull him out!

In 1949, eleven-year-old Derryl Ruppert of Akron aroused attention for two reasons. His car was uniquely covered with papier-mâché, and *he* was the smallest con-

*The 1947 Derby winner, Kenneth Holmboe of Charleston, West Virginia, had a problem squeezing his long frame into his racer.*

testant in the history of the All-American, weighing only fifty-seven pounds. He was quite a contrast to another contestant in the race, fifteen-year-old Howard Kermode of Los Angeles, who at 150 pounds and 5′ 11″ was one of the largest. Howard dieted to keep his weight down, then on the day of the race drank *thirty* bottles of milk to bring it up to the maximum allowed. He had tried to save weight by building his car of aluminum and light wood; his measurements were so close that, as the newspaper reported, he "almost had to be eased into the car with a shoehorn."

The 1955 winner, Dick Rohrer of Rochester, New York, also had a problem because of height. At fourteen, he was six feet tall, more than one foot taller than most of the other 153 champs. While he was building his racer he grew eight inches and couldn't get into it, so he had to build a second one. He probably didn't mind building another car—he seemingly loved building racers, having constructed his first one at age nine, using the wheels of his own baby buggy.

Another boy whose height gave him difficulty was 1958 winner James Miley, fifteen, of Muncie, Indiana. He had spent almost a year building his very low car. For many weeks before the race, he did bending exercises because he knew he would find it hard to squeeze his 6′ 1″ frame into his racer.

Jim was one of the fortunate boys who attended a special thirteen-week Derby school in Muncie, Indiana. The school,

*James Miley of Muncie, Indiana, 1958 champion. From left to right are Ohio Governor C. William O'Neill, Akron Mayor Leo Berg, Jim's sister, his mother, and Edward Cole, vice-president of General Motors.*

run by Bob Turner, winner of the first All-American Soap Box Derby, taught the boys the finer points of engineering and the art of building racers. It turned out many champions.

The 1959 winner, Barney Townsend, thirteen, of Anderson, Indiana, was very serious and quiet, a "loner." Perhaps he felt self-conscious because he was small for his age:

*Terry Townsend, 1957 champion, with his mother and father, younger brother Barney (standing), and older brother Brooks, 1955 local champion of Anderson, Indiana.*

5' 2½" and 97 pounds. But after winning the race (by a length), his emotions were released and he burst into tears. The whole family joined him, crying with joy! They knew how hard he had worked, using all his spare time to build *two* racers, trying them both out, and choosing the better one. Barney made Derby history by being the brother of 1957 winner Terry Townsend. It was the first time that brothers had won the number one spot in the All-American.

In 1974 Curt Yarborough from Elk Grove, California, won in a car almost identical to the one in which his brother Brett won in the 1973 Derby. They were the first brothers to be back-to-back champs. The two brothers got tips on building a winning racer from Larry Blair, the 1971 national champion from nearby Oroville, California.

Soap box racer drivers come from a variety of backgrounds. In the early days of the Derby in particular, during the Depression, some of them came from very poor homes. In 1937 the Memphis champ, who was fatherless and one of nine children, wore his first pair of shoes when he arrived in Akron. He bought them with the $6.50 he had won at his local derby race. Perhaps because he felt more comfortable that way, he raced barefoot.

Two contestants from Georgia that year attracted a lot of attention: Hugh Flury and Joe Wood. Hugh Flury, a small twelve-year-old from Atlanta, had been disqualified the year before because the judges didn't think someone that *small* could build a racer by himself. He didn't take any chances when he built his "Georgia Headache," and had lots of witnesses to prove that he did the work. He placed fifth in the 1937 race, which was an especially exciting one, with 120 contestants and 100,000 spectators.

Joe Wood, who came from a farm near Columbus, Georgia, named his racer "Rhett Butler," in honor of the character in the popular book *Gone with the Wind*. He had gotten the idea for the design of his car by watching a drop of water falling from a faucet, studying its shape, and designing his car like it—elongated at the ends. Both Georgia boys complained because the hotel didn't serve their favorite meal, grits and biscuits.

Another farm boy was Herman Goehring, from Boise, Idaho, who got up at 5 A.M. each day to milk the cows and do chores. When he arrived at the 1940 Derby, the automobile he rode in was decorated in a unique way. The whole front of the car was covered with potatoes, and with a big sign reading: "Here Comes Idaho."

Quite a few farm boys have participated in the Derby. The Los Angeles champion in 1946 was Dave Smith, who lived in Arcadia, California. He earned the money for his racer ($15.60) by milking cows. And in 1951 the crowd got quite a kick out of the Milwaukee champ when he arrived in a truck, milking a cow.

The 1949 Derby saw some interestingly dressed contestants. San Diego champ John Panuelas proudly displayed his Mexican heritage by wearing a high sombrero and beautifully decorated silk shirt and trousers. Rudy Meier came from Alaska dressed in a parka. Sweltering in Akron's

*Celebrities who attended the 1963 Derby: Rock Hudson, Paul Anka, Arthur Godfrey, Paul Lynde, and John Russell.*

heat, he paid frequent trips to the soda fountain to cool off! Lloyd Wetenkamp of Casper, Wyoming, arrived in a cowboy suit and boots.

The 1950 Derby crowd gave a big welcome to a former contestant, Eugene Diggs, who was the 1948 Detroit winner. Eugene had pedaled 200 miles in the rain to root for the 1950 Detroit champ! Newspaper photographers swarmed over him, and as a result of this publicity, his bike was shipped back and he was given a ride home.

Philip Raber, from Sugarcreek, Ohio (60 miles south of Akron), made Derby history in 1976 by being the first world's championship winner in the new Junior Division. Sugarcreek paid him a great honor when they held their annual Swiss festival that fall. The festival parade led off with a float featuring Phil "driving" his racer. There were carnival rides and a Swiss contest in which competitors threw a stone weighing 138 pounds. (Phil passed up *that* contest.) He returned to Akron in 1977 as the Senior Division contestant from Sugarcreek.

One of the biggest boons Soap Box Derby contestants seem to have is the unusually close support given them by their families. Parents have shown an amazing tolerance for the way their houses have been thrown into disarray. A reporter in a 1937 newspaper article told about overhearing, in a conversation between the mothers of Derby contestants: "John built his car in my sewing room, and when he had it finished couldn't get it out the door."

And the father of Harold Zoellner, who raced in the 1940 Derby, was quite surprised when he went down to the basement of his Cape Girardeau, Missouri, home to fix his furnace. "Where's the furnace pipe?" he yelled up the stairs.

"I used it to make the body of my racer," Harold called back.

Then there was 1951 Derby winner Darwin Cooper, whose mother permitted him to build his racer in the dining room of their Danville, Pennsylvania, home. He would have worked in the garage, but the garage was being rebuilt. When Darwin finally went to Akron, four car-loads of friends accompanied him and his parents!

A very touching relationship was that between 1962 winner David Mann of Gary, Indiana, and his grand-mother. Slim, ninety-pound, bespectacled David was given much help by "Marm." She cleaned out a room for him to work in and gave him encouragement as he worked on his car. She scrimped and saved to buy him power tools. Most important of all, she kept up his courage when he was ready to quit. Perhaps this was why he didn't give up when he was trailing halfway down the track; he drove a bullet-straight heat and nosed out the other two racers.

An especially close family were the Yarboroughs, who produced two Derby winners: Brett in 1973 and Curt in 1974. The Yarboroughs lived on a farm, and their father thought one of the reasons for his sons' success was all the practice they had had driving tractors.

A poignant scene took place in the 1977 Derby. Jeff Townsend, twelve, of Anderson, Indiana, raced in a car he called "Dad's Dream." His father, 1959 All-American champ Barney Townsend, had died that June. His Uncle Terry, who had won in 1957, had helped him finish the racer. Jeff shed no tears at his narrow defeat, but bravely said, "I did the best I could." His grandfather and uncle were more emotionally shaken.

*Curtis Yarborough of Elk Grove, California, was the 1974 champion. Standing behind him are his father; Ron Baker, the general manager of the All-American that year; and his mother. Beside him are his brother Brett, 1973 champion, and his sister.*

Also participating in the 1977 Derby was the Ferdinand family of Canton, Ohio. The Ferdinand parents and all five children, three girls and two boys, had long been involved in Derby events. A wall in their home is filled with trophies of the children's winning races. The two top winners were Joan, who won the Senior Division championship in 1976, and Mark, who won the Junior Division

*Barney Townsend of Anderson, Indiana, 1959 champion, with his father, mother, Vice-President Richard Nixon, and Edward Cole, vice-president of General Motors. The brother of 1957 champion Terry Townsend, Barney made history as it was the first time brothers had won the number one spot.*

*1977 Junior Division champion Mark Ferdinand. With him are Tom Kilroy, executive vice-president of Novar Electronics; his sister Joan, who was 1976 Senior Division champion; and his mother and father.*

championship in 1977. The Ferdinands are such ardent soap box racing fans that when they're not participating in the program in Akron, they're traveling hundreds of miles to attend numerous soap box racing rallies.

Every year the All-American Soap Box Derby has a new "cast of characters," since a contestant may race only one time each in the Junior Division and Senior Division. They still range from small size to large size, with a variety of different abilities and regional accents. But once they get together in Derbytown, where they live during Derby week, differences are forgotten. They act the way Derby groups have always acted, making new friends, playing mild jokes on one another, and just plain having fun!

# 7 ☆ Dark Days
# for the Derby

Derby officials have always tried to make the races fair by keeping out cheaters. Unfortunately, some participants have resorted to "dirty tricks." Some have been disqualified for lying about their age or having someone else build the racer for them. Some have tried weighing in with lightweight clothes and, before starting the race, switching to heavy shoes. Some have tried to sneak weights in their pockets. A favorite trick was to wear sneakers at the official weigh-in and then change to steel-tipped boots.

Some have tried to secrete chunks of metal, bricks, or cement in their cars because a heavy car is better able to overcome wind resistance. One driver tried releasing a bowling ball from between his legs so it would hit the nose of the car and give it an extra boost! Despite their ingenuity, the participants using these illegal ways to win have usually been caught.

The nation was shocked, therefore, in 1973 when headlines in newspapers across the country screamed the news that, for the first time in the history of the All-American

Soap Box Derby, the *winner* had cheated! Jimmy Gronen, fourteen, of Boulder, Colorado, had been declared winner. His friends were particularly eager for Jimmy to win because he had suffered quite a bit of misfortune in his family life. His father had died of a stroke in 1967, when Jimmy was eight. His mother had kept her three children together for five years, until she became ill and had to be hospitalized. Jimmy's younger brother and sister went to live with one of their mother's sisters, and Jimmy went to live with the other one, in Colorado. His aunt had married Robert Lange, well-to-do owner of the Lange Ski Boot Corporation.

Lange had raced in his local soap box derby as a boy. His son, Robert Lange, Jr., had won first place in the 1972 Derby. When Jimmy expressed interest in building a soap box racer, the Langes were delighted. According to Mr. Lange, Jimmy spent many hours working on his racer at the Lange factory.

On August 19, 1973, at the thirty-sixth running of the All-American Soap Box Derby, James Gronen was affectionately called "Big Jim." This was because of his small size: 68 pounds and 4' 4" tall. Jimmy carried a pocket knife as a lucky charm for about half of the race, then gave it away when he decided it was too heavy. He didn't even know he had won, he said, until he heard the announcement during the final championship heat. "I concentrated on my own car. I didn't even see the other car. I was looking dead ahead."

Jimmy Gronen wasn't to keep the championship title

very long, however. Suspicions were first aroused when his sleek, torpedo-shaped racer jumped to an unusually quick getaway down the sloping 954-foot course. Nothing but the force of gravity is supposed to propel the soap box racers, yet Jimmy's racer sped to a lead of several tenths of a second in a race rarely won by more than two tenths of a second!

Onlookers took movies of the extremely quick starts of the Gronen car and showed them to the officials. The films showed the nose of the car staying closer to the steel starting plate upon release than did the noses of other cars.

The Derby officials themselves were suspicious when Jimmy ran one heat 20/100ths of a second faster than any other car in the field, according to Derby general manager Paul Livick. "That raised some eyebrows. Especially when you run computerized wheels. And there were a lot of cars in there with the same basic body design as that Boulder car. There should not really be that much of a difference. Maybe a couple of hundredths of a second, but not twenty hundredths."

There was curiosity, too, as to why Jimmy Gronen's times had worsened with each heat:

| | |
|---|---|
| First heat | 27.48 seconds |
| Semifinal | 27.63 seconds |
| Final | 27.68 seconds |

Normally, as the tires warm up, heat times get progressively faster. After the race, a special examination of the car was set up. A Derby inspector found a small button in the headrest. He drilled through and found wires and a battery. This accounted for Jimmy's car's being slower each trip down the hill: the battery was being drained! The car was taken to Goodyear Aerospace, near Derby Downs, and X-rayed. It was discovered that an electro-magnet in the nose had been connected to the battery in the rear of the racer.

When cars are lined up at the raceway, the nose of each car rests flush against a hinged metal plate that drops forward down the inclined track. Jimmy Gronen's helmet touched off a lever that activated the battery and magnet. As the metal plate fell forward, the magnet's pull toward it gave the car enough extra starting force to win. The magnet had been overlooked in the inspection of the car because it had been built into the nose. In the old days the frames of the cars could be opened up to look inside, but the Gronen car had a fiberglass body so it wasn't possible to see inside it.

The Akron Chamber of Commerce announced the news about the magnet and about Jimmy's disqualification. Brett Yarborough, eleven, of Elk Grove, California, who had come in second, was declared the new champion. Each of the following eight finishers was moved up a notch.

The Akron *Beacon Journal*, which had been a loyal supporter of the All-American since its move to Akron in 1935, said in an editorial: "Just because one winning

*James Gronen, declared world champion in the 1973 Derby, was later disqualified when an illegal magnet was discovered in the nose of his racer.*

*Brett Yarborough of Elk Grove, California, became winner of the 1973 Derby when James Gronen was disqualified.*

horse was given illegal medication at the Kentucky Derby . . . the integrity of that classic was not impugned. It should be the same in Akron with the All-American."

Jimmy Gronen's uncle, Robert Lange, issued a statement saying that he had *urged* Jimmy to use the magnet because so many others were cheating, too. Lange demanded that the other eight winning cars in the 1973 Derby be inspected. They were examined and found to be "clean."

Boulder, Colorado, District Attorney Alex Hunter was outraged. He filed charges against Lange in juvenile court for encouraging a youngster to violate the law. When the case finally came before a Boulder juvenile court judge, he ordered Lange to pay a $2,000 fine, which was given to the Boulder Boys' Club. The judge also ordered Lange to apologize to the nation's youth and banned him from all Soap Box Derby operations for two years.

Ohio Summit County prosecutor Stephen M. Gabalac was so stunned by the besmirching of the All-American Soap Box Derby that he made a remark that was widely quoted in many newspapers and magazines: "It's like seeing apple pie, motherhood, and the American flag grinding to a halt."

All sorts of rumors started flying around, especially in view of the fact that Jimmy Gronen had won in a car that was almost identical to the one his cousin Bobby Lange had raced to win the 1972 Derby. According to Derby rules, the Lange car, as a winning racer, was supposed to remain in Akron. By some oversight, it had been shipped back to Boulder.

People demanded that it be returned to Akron for inspection. Mystery was now added to the Lange case as while the Langes were on vacation after the scandal about Jimmy's magnet broke, Bobby's car disappeared! Lange said it had been stolen from the basement and that there had not been a magnet in it.

It was rumored that the Lange cars had cost over $20,000 to build, that they had been constructed by an expert at the ski boot factory, and that they had been tested in a wind tunnel. Lange issued a denial. He said Jimmy and Bobby had built their own cars and no significant expense went into them. He had aided the boys only in the permissible area of "advice and counsel." He readily admitted that Bobby's car had been tested in a wind tunnel but said there was nothing in the rule book prohibiting this.

Charges and counter-charges were flung back and forth. Andy Noyes, father of third-place winner Chris Noyes, said, "Let's give the Derby back to the kids, where it belongs."

One of those kids, David Abramovitz, fifteen, of Oak Forest, Illinois, knew what the Derby is really all about. He said, "If you cheat and win, well, it seems to me, did you *really* win?"

# 8 ☆ The Derby Starts Rebuilding

The scandal of 1973 had tarnished the name of the All-American Soap Box Derby. The "biggest amateur racing event in the world" had lost the confidence of its public. The number of participating cities had dropped from a high of 272 in 1972 to 100 in 1974.

Previous to this, in 1972, the All-American had suffered a financial setback when Chevrolet, after thirty-five years, dropped its sponsorship. The Akron Chamber of Commerce obtained the rights from Chevrolet and sponsored the 1973 Derby, but on December 28, 1973, cut its ties with the All-American. The next month the Akron Jaycees (Junior Chamber of Commerce) formed a "Save the All-American Committee." This committee, which evolved into International Soap Box Derby, Inc., was headed by Ron D. Baker and composed of Akron Jaycees and other Ohio businessmen.

General Manager Ron D. Baker and his small staff had to face the challenge of rebuilding the good name of the All-American Soap Box Derby. Baker was confident that

*Ronald D. Baker, who was general manager of the All-American Soap Box Derby from 1974 to 1977.*

"a new and better Derby would rise from the ashes of the old one." New starting blocks would render any magnet ineffective, Baker said, and "new realistic and enforceable rules are now in effect."

The new 1974 rules stated that the contestants had to demonstrate their skills by answering questions from the inspectors about the construction of their racers. In some cases, they had to duplicate steps in the construction of their cars. Twenty-three out of ninety-nine cars were tested to see whether the contestants had built the cars themselves. Some were disqualified for safety reasons. It was also ruled that the insides of the cars "from nose to tail" must be accessible to permit inspection for such things as magnets.

More rules have been put into writing since then to make sure that every contestant gets a fair chance to win. The local sponsor now has to fill out a form attesting that:

> "The Soap Box Derby racer of the champ to be entered in the All-American Soap Box Derby was constructed by the champ in all respects in accordance with the official rules governing the All-American Soap Box Derby. This form is to be signed by the Derby Director, local champ, and parents or guardians.
>
> "The racer must be shipped, transported, or delivered to Derby Downs, Akron, Ohio, by members of the local race committee or persons designated by them who are *not* members of the champion's family. Parents or members of the champion's family in no instance may transport or deliver a Soap Box Derby racer. Following the All-American, the Soap Box Derby racer (unless it is one of the three top finishers) will be returned to the local Soap Box Derby committee."

The Soap Box Derby Rule Book says that "entrant must build car. You must perform all the work in building your racer. You may have help in the areas outlined:

A. Design and planning
B. Layout of floorboard

C. Setting up power tools
D. Brake
E. Drilling of axles and steering shaft
F. Steering
G. Holding heavy components
H. Mixing of fiberglass, resins, plastics, and paint
 I. Alignment . . ."

The 1974 race was a success, even though it was smaller than previous races. The following year the International

*1977 Senior Division champion Steve Washburn of Bristol, Connecticut. With him are James Ott, president of Novar Electronics; his mother; F. A. Wahl, chairman of the board of trustees, International Soap Box Derby, Inc.; and his father.*

Soap Box Derby, Inc., again ran the program. In November of 1975 the Derby got some very encouraging news. Novar Electronics Corporation, a leading producer of electronic security equipment, offered to become a sponsor. It was the first time since 1972 that the All-American had a national sponsor.

The other exciting event that occurred in 1976 was the establishment of a Junior Division, giving youngsters ten through twelve a kit to purchase from the All-American and a class of their own to race in. Philip Raber, eleven, of Sugarcreek, Ohio, became the first Kit Car champion, beating a field of sixty other Junior Division contestants.

The 1976 Derby was a big success, attracting over 15,000 people. This 39th All-American was especially colorful because it had been declared an official Bicentennial event, and so was permitted to use the Bicentennial symbol and flag for its decorations. It literally started with a *bang*. Seven members from Pitts Battery, Munroe Falls, Ohio, who were dressed in colonial costumes, rolled a 200-year-old, 6-pound cannon to the top of the track. The cannon went off with an earsplitting roar, shocking everyone into complete silence.

In 1978 the All-American Soap Box Derby got a new general manager, Wayne L. Alley. Novar Electronics continued its sponsorship. The Derby was given another boost in 1978 with the introduction of senior Kit Cars, which were so well received that 650 raced and 38 made it to the All-American that year.

The future of the All-American Soap Box Derby looked

*Mark Ferdinand, junior champion of the 1977 Derby, in his winning racer.*

*From left to right are James Ott, president of Novar Electronics Corp., national sponsor of the All-American Soap Box Derby; Frank Wahl, chairman of the board of International Soap Box Derby, Inc.; and Wayne L. Alley, general manager of the All-American Soap Box Derby.*

bright to its Chairman of the National Control Board, Bill Ford: "Rule changes are improving the Derby program. There is not so much concentrated knowledge or expertise about car building. It used to be that so-called secrets of how to balance weight, align cars, etc., were known only by a few people throughout the country. Today, through programs such as the Kit Cars, everyone has access to basically the same type information. We believe that today's rules and other information about how to build cars are a big factor in equalizing chances for everyone."

# 9 ☆ How to Get Started

Perhaps you are already a participant in this exciting sport. Or maybe you would like to be one and want to learn how you can become a soap box racer driver. If there is no local Soap Box Derby Association in your area, you may write for information to:

> The All-American Soap Box Derby
> 789 Derby Downs Drive
> Akron, Ohio 44306

You may want to subscribe to *Topside*, their interesting monthly newsletter.

The All-American has very high standards, as explained in their Official Rule Books. The Official Rule Book for the Junior Division starts off by explaining the program:

"The Junior Division Kit Car program is designed as a parent-child program. A parent or adult is expected to help in the construction of the car. The adult is not to

Trial run taken by Jeff Iula, now of the Derby staff, in the 1966 Derby. Because of an airline strike, the boy from Okinawa could not get to the United States so Jeff substituted for him.

build the car for the boy or the girl but to share this experience by being there and giving help only if and when needed. This program is meant to be an enjoyable learning experience for both parent and child, and to provide them with the opportunity to develop mutual respect, trust, and demonstrate the importance of individual pride and sportsmanship."

The Junior Division Soap Box Derby is limited to ages ten through twelve. You must enter and participate in the local race that is closest to where you live. Twelve-year-olds have the choice of racing in either the Junior or Senior Division, but if you race in the Junior Division you must use a Kit Car.

Your Kit Car has to be purchased from the All-American Soap Box Derby, and you must drive the racer you build. Except for the steps outlined in the Rule Book, you must perform all of the work in building your racer. For safety reasons, you are required to wear trousers, shirt, tennis shoes, and a helmet when racing. The following are grounds for disqualification:

1. Unsafe racer.
2. The use of graphite, chemicals, pumice or powder in any form, on or in the car, on or in the wheels, or on any part of the driver's body or clothing is prohibited.
3. Poor sportsmanship.
4. Any attempt to gain unfair advantage.

The car may not be wider than 24 inches or longer than 80 inches. The combined weight of car and driver cannot exceed 220 pounds for Junior Division contestants. Only unaltered ¾-inch official Soap Box Derby axles provided in the Junior Kit may be used. You must make your car available for periodic inspections as required by your local Derby Director during construction.

This is just a sampling of the information contained in the Rule Book. The All-American is constantly striving to make soap box racing as safe as possible and to make sure that each contestant has an equal chance of winning. They are happy with the response to the Kit Car program, which has enabled many boys and girls with limited mechanical ability to participate in the sport of soap box car racing.

The Senior Division has its own Rule Book. Twelve-through fifteen-year-olds are eligible. Some of the same rules listed in the Junior Division book apply to the seniors. Of course the dimensions of the junior and senior cars differ, and there is much detail given on building a Senior Division car. Because of the success of the Junior Kit Car program, a Senior Kit Car program was introduced in 1978. It was enthusiastically received.

If there is a local soap box derby association in your area, you are very fortunate. The local derby associations conduct a series of clinics in the construction of soap box racers, and they will give you all the help you need. If

*Kim Watts, 1975 Derby contestant, getting her car inspected.*

there is no derby association nearby, perhaps another soap box racing group can help you:

National Derby Rallies
3 Gregory Lane
Lexington, Illinois 61753

The National Derby Rallies' rules are quite informal. The driver of the car does not have to be its builder. There is no pre-inspection of cars, no rules about clothing, and the age limits are flexible. Local races are held in different parts of the country, usually in the spring and fall months. The rallies give the young drivers additional opportunity to race.

It is believed that the first rally was held in 1969 in Anderson, Indiana, between the towns of Anderson and Lafayette, with forty-six boys and girls participating. The rallies have grown rapidly in popularity, with many families traveling hundreds of miles to attend regional races.

The National Derby Rallies are held annually, usually the week after the All-American in Akron. The first national championship race was run in 1977 in Warren, Ohio, which is about an hour's ride from Akron. It was won by Shelly Brower of Newbury Park, California. The 1978 National Derby Rally was held in Columbus, Ohio. The Senior Division winner was Jeff Murphy of Elk Grove, California.

Over and over again one hears from soap box racing

*In the 1979 Derby, Russ Yurk of Flint, Michigan, was Junior Division winner.*

*Craig Kitchen of Akron, Ohio, was Senior Division winner in the 1979 Derby.*

*The Derby always concludes with an awards show. Shown here are the 1979 winners, with the Kitchen family on the left and the Yurk family on the right.*

contestants that they particularly like this sport because "the kids and their parents really try to *help* one another. Sure, we all want to win, but when one of us is in trouble, the others try to help."

It's that kind of spirit that makes soap box racing so much fun!

# 10 ☆ Gayle Goes to Akron

Gayle Kermode rubbed her eyes tiredly as she got off the plane at the Akron airport on August 6, 1978. It was now midafternoon, and she had risen at 4 A.M. that Sunday morning to catch the 7:30 A.M. plane from Los Angeles International Airport. There had been a stopover in Chicago to make connections with the plane to Akron.

It was not her first visit to Akron, but this time was different. This time, she was coming as a soap box racing champion, winner of the 1978 Los Angeles County Soap Box Derby. This time, she had a chance to win the biggest prize in the soap box racing world: the championship in the All-American Soap Box Derby!

Gayle was accompanied by her mother, father, and brother. Arriving in Akron, they caught a cab to their hotel, where they stayed overnight. The forty-first running of the All-American Soap Box Derby (it was not held during the war years 1942–1945) was to be held the following Saturday, August 12, but there was to be an exciting schedule of activities preceding it.

It has always been the tradition of the All-American to

treat its young champions (of their local derbies) like royalty. On Monday the champs were picked up individually by limousines and driven, with an escort of police motorcycles, to downtown Akron. As they alighted from the automobiles, their names were announced over the loudspeaker.

Members of a school band accompanied them up a red carpet onto a stage, where a giant-sized book had been placed. Like the other boys and girls, Gayle signed her

*Gayle Kermode of Glendale, California, signs in for the 1978 Derby. The number 49 in the corner of the book was the number assigned to her racer.*

name and city in the book. Photographs were taken and each champion was given an official All-American T-shirt and hat. As the crowd applauded, the youngsters threw mementos to them: buttons, balloons, or whatever small souvenirs they had. This welcoming ceremony goes back to early Derby history.

The contestants then got into three big buses and, led by police cars with screeching sirens, were driven to Camp Y-Noah (Derbytown), fifteen miles south of Akron, where they were to stay until race day. The "Y" camp, adjacent to a freshwater lake, provided a variety of recreational sports: swimming, boating, hiking, horseback riding, baseball, and basketball. There were all sorts of table games and activities improvised by the camp counselors. And, of course, all sorts of horseplay, thought up by the boys and girls themselves!

The next day, Tuesday, the contestants had to go to Topside for the official inspection and weigh-in. Topside is the building at the top of the Derby Downs hill where the champs' cars are inspected and stored. No parents are allowed inside the Topside area, and security is maintained by armed policemen from two weeks before the race to one week after.

Gayle's racer had been weighed on a bathroom scale before being shipped to Akron. She needed to add only a six-ounce lead weight to come up to the maximum of 250 pounds. All racers and drivers were weighed again on race day and before every heat.

*Having fun at Derbytown Camp before the 1979 races are local champions Jennifer Clark of Chattanooga, Tennessee, (left) and Prudence Short of Charleston, West Virginia.*

Wednesday was an especially busy day. The contestants returned to Derby Downs for trial runs. A crew from NBC's television program "America Alive" did a live segment of the trial runs. Also appearing in it was world-famous soccer player Pélé, who visited with the champions and signed autographs for them.

Wednesday was important, also, for the critical task of alignment of axles. Each contestant was allowed twenty minutes to line up the axle spindles. Two helpers were

*Gayle Kermode, representing Los Angeles County in the 1978 All-American, is in lane 2 at the starting ramp.*

allowed in the pit area to help align the racer, so Gayle Kermode's father and brother helped her. A downpour of rain occurred during alignment and they had to run for cover, but officials permitted them to return the next day to finish the job. At 7:30 Wednesday evening the cars were put on public display.

Thursday afternoon was open house at Derbytown for the parents. There were more visitors to the camp Friday: actress Patti Weaver of the TV serial "Days of Our Lives" and actor Bobby Troup of TV's "Emergency!" Saturday, race day, the boys and girls were bussed back to Derby Downs.

Derby Downs was constructed in 1936 on the outskirts of Akron, across from the Akron Municipal Airport. Sometimes, when races are in progress, airplanes fly over the track—paper airplanes from children sitting in the stands and real airplanes from the airfield. Originally the track was 2,000 feet long, with a racing distance of 1,175 feet. In 1940 it was shortened to 1,000 feet because the better-designed racing cars were going too fast. It was shortened again in 1946, to 975 feet, and again in 1971, to 953 feet.

Permanent grandstands were installed, as were a garage with service facilities and a triple-deck bridge. The bridge is over the finish line. As each racer crosses the finish line, it breaks an electric-eye beam that triggers a special camera and timing clock. In a close race, the photo-finish negative can be developed and projected on a screen to help the judges decide who the winner is.

The track is 30 feet wide with a 1,200-foot run-out area beyond the finish line. Its macadam surface has been specially painted to reduce glare. It is bordered by rubber-surfaced retaining walls. Parallel lines running down the full length of the track help the drivers stay in the correct lane. The track starts with a 16 percent grade, then gradually drops off to 6 percent, and is nearly level at the finish line. Derby Downs is kept in good condition to make it safe and fair for contestants.

First-round heats for the All-American are established by drawing the names of sponsoring cities on the Monday preceding race day. The first name drawn is in heat 1, lane 1; second name, heat 1, lane 2; and third name, heat 1, lane 3. Heats with only two cars use lanes 1 and 3. The heat winners, from the first round on, draw for lane positions for the heats in the next round. After round 1, each succeeding round narrows down the field. In the final round, the top three winners race for the All-American championship. Prizes and trophies are awarded to the top nine finishers in each division.

Flags are important in directing the races. The checkered flag designates the heat winner. The green flag means the track is clear, while the red flag signals "stop—track not clear."

Every All-American Soap Box Derby starts off with a parade. This pre-game event lends much excitement to the Derby, for the parades are always colorful and interesting to watch. They have attracted celebrities from many different walks of life. In 1935 Tom Mix, the famous hero of the Western movies, participated. So did Eddie Rickenbacker, the World War I flying ace, a former automobile racing driver. Lieutenant-General James H. Doolittle, hero of the World War II raid on Tokyo, appeared in the tenth anniversary celebration in 1947.

In 1950 the first Oil Can Trophy Race was held. In this event, adult celebrities "race" each other in oversized Derby cars. Jack Dempsey, former heavyweight boxing champion, had been invited to appear in the Oil Can Race. When he looked down the long slope at Derby Downs, he gave a mock shudder. "I'd rather climb into the ring with Tunney

*Many celebrities attended the 1950 Derby. From left to right are William Boyd (Hopalong Cassidy), movie star James Stewart, former world champion boxer Jack Dempsey, a General Motors representative, and Indianapolis Speedway champion Wilbur Shaw.*

than go down that hill," he said. (Tunney had beaten him for the world's heavyweight championship.) He later relented, however, and raced actor Jimmy Stewart and three-time Indianapolis Speedway winner Wilbur Shaw. Dempsey, driving a bright blue racer with double wheels in the rear, won!

Jimmy Stewart made his *fifth* Derby appearance in 1952. Also appearing that year were Edgar Bergen, the popular ventriloquist, with his almost-human little "friend" Charlie McCarthy. When the track was so soaked with rain that the start of the 1953 Derby was held up, singer Dinah Shore entertained the audience for twenty-nine minutes.

TV's "Bonanza" stars had a gleeful time participating in the 1962 Oil Can Trophy Race. Lorne Greene thanked his TV sons, Dan Blocker and Michael Landon, for letting him win! Since 1962 marked the silver anniversary of the Derby, there was a particularly large celebration, which delayed the first heat for seventy minutes.

*The traditional oil-can race of celebrities at the 1979 Derby. Celebrities at the 1979 Derby were actors Charlene Tilton, George Takei, Richard Paul, and Peter Fonda, seen here with Derby general manager Wayne L. Alley.*

The Derby has also had politicians as guest participants. In 1959, then Vice-President Richard Nixon attended the race. In 1967 Ohio Governor James Rhodes led off the parade, which included Akron Mayor John Ballard.

The 1978 Derby festivities, in which Gayle Kermode was to participate, started at 11 A.M. with a hot-air balloon race. Then three parachute jumpers landed on the track. After they left, the parade began. It featured former world champs, bands and marching groups from Akron and surrounding areas, and the most important people of all: the 169 local champions who were to race that day. The champions, Gayle among them, marched down the track, proudly wearing the All-American official helmet and racing jacket and carrying their sponsoring city's flag.

Following the parade, there were two Oil Can Trophy races. In one heat, singer John Raitt and actor Bobby Troup were beaten by actress Patti Weaver. In a second race, Los Angeles Kings hockey player Dave Gardner defeated Cleveland Cavaliers basketball player John Lambert and actress Char Fontane.

Next, John Raitt sang the song "Impossible Dream," from the play *Man of La Mancha*. Raitt dedicated the song to the champs, who he said had achieved *their* "impossible dream" by becoming contestants in the All-American. Then, after "The Star-Spangled Banner" was played, a Revolutionary War cannon was fired, signaling the start of the race.

The first heat of the Senior Division left the starting

gates at about 1 P.M. The Senior and Junior Division rounds ran alternately throughout the afternoon.

At Topside, when Gayle and her car were weighed on the scales by the Derby officials, she was almost two pounds over the maximum weight. She took a large piece of lead out of her racer, and the scale then read "250." Her car was rolled along the concrete floor and put into the lineup of cars. There were three lines, one for each lane.

She waited quietly for her number to be called. This was a single elimination race, which meant she had only one

*Gayle Kermode, 1978 All-American Soap Box Derby contestant, waiting to get her car weighed.*

chance to win each time she went down the hill. She would need some luck, along with her skill, because though the Akron officials do an excellent job of matching lanes and wheels, it is impossible to keep the lanes equal. As the race proceeds, the temperature and sun cause changes in the lanes.

When Gayle heard her number called, she fastened her helmet and moved under the red, white, and blue metal Topside arch. With the help of a handler, she began easing her car down to the starting blocks, 250 feet below. She had hold of the front end of the car, and the handler, using metal hooks, held the rear of the car. He asked her if she thought she would win.

She replied modestly, "I doubt it." He told her he thought she would, as almost everyone in lane 2 had won so far.

The Derby official directed heat number 23 to put their cars into the starting blocks. Gayle and the other two drivers checked the placement of their wheels and got into their cars. Gayle had lane 2. Ken Walker of Durham, North Carolina, was in lane 1, and Mike Manderacchi of Conshohocken, Pennsylvania, was in lane 3. The starter waved a green flag, the starting blocks dropped, and they were off!

Gayle didn't hear the roar of the crowd; she was too busy trying to adjust to the unfamiliar track. She felt herself swerving, and it made her angry. She also thought about the boy in the adjacent lane who had been teasing her all week at camp on how he was going to beat her. "I've *got*

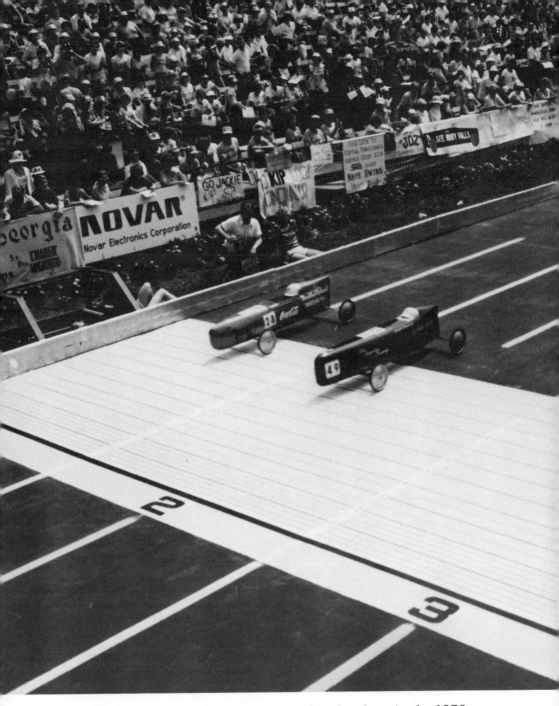

*Gayle Kermode in lane 2, at the start of her first heat in the 1978 Derby.*

to win!" she said to herself. And she did—by 18 inches. Her time was 27.61 seconds. Ken Walker was second and Mike Manderacchi, third.

Her car was put onto a truck to be taken back up the hill for her next heat. The losing cars were moved to one side where their official gold racing wheels were replaced with their own red wheels. They were then put alongside a storage shed, to be picked up later by their owners. The losing contestants were comforted by the "Y" counselors, who escorted them to a special location in the grandstand. From there, they cheered on their friends who were still in the race.

Gayle and her car went back to the scales for another weigh-in and then back into line to wait for her next heat, number 37, to be called. While she was waiting, David Collins, her Regional Derby Director, went over to talk to her. He remarked about her swerving, which she took as a warning that "I might not be as lucky in this next heat as I was the first time."

In round 2, Gayle was again in lane 2. Jimmy Giles of Racine, Wisconsin, was in lane 1, and Dean Huminsky of Western Pennsylvania was in lane 3. "When we started racing," said Gayle, "I could see that both the other cars were ahead of me. I began getting scared and held my steering wheel as straight as I could. In the last fifty feet of the track, my racer started gaining speed. It was really close! I had to wait fifteen minutes for them to examine the photo-finish photograph, but at last they announced I

had won. If I had swerved one more time or my opponents
had swerved one less time, I would have lost!" Her winning
time was 27.6 seconds. The photo showed that Gayle had
beaten Dean Huminsky by less than one inch!

Gayle was now in the top nine. The next round would
determine which racers would advance to the heats for
first-second-third, fourth-fifth-sixth, or seventh-eighth-ninth
places. In round 3, heat number 42, Gayle had lane 3.
Lane 3 was the slow lane now as the shadows began to
fall on that part of the track. In this heat she swerved
slightly and ended up second by ten inches to Bob Bemis
of Owosso, Michigan. This placed Gayle in the heat for
fourth-fifth-sixth places. Bob Bemis went on to gain third
place in the final heat, just behind second-place winner
A. J. Simonds of San Francisco.

"After coming in second in my third heat," Gayle said,
"I started feeling bad. On the way back up to Topside on
the truck, I was silent. Some man asked me if I was okay.
I said, 'Yes,' even though I felt sick to my stomach. I felt
bad because I knew that there was no way now that I could
win first place."

In heat number 44, her final heat, Gayle raced another
girl, Laurie Sheetz from Lower Bucks County, Pennsylvania, and Carl Mace from Stark County, Ohio. The other
cars had faster times, and Gayle was third in this heat,
making her the overall sixth-place winner.

At Topside, after the race, the nine top finishers
were photographed and congratulated. Gregory Cardinal,

*Gregory Cardinal of Flint, Michigan, was Senior Division winner in the 1978 Derby.*

thirteen, of Flint, Michigan, was the winner of the Senior Division with a winning time of 27.61 seconds. Gayle wished she were in his place!

When the Kermodes returned to their hotel, Gayle, who had withstood the pressure of racing remarkably well, broke down and cried. Her father tried to console her. "Gayle, think of all the hundreds of boys and girls throughout this country—and some foreign ones—who race. And *you* raced against the best of them all at the All-American and placed sixth. Why, we're proud of you!"

The closing event of Derby week was the awards ceremony, which took place at seven o'clock that night at the Akron Civic Theater. James Ott, president of Novar Electronics, the Derby's national sponsor, handed out the prizes. First-place Senior Division winner Greg Cardinal received a $3,000 college scholarship; second-place winner A. J. Simonds, a $2,000 scholarship; and third-place winner Bob Bemis, $1,000. As one of the fourth-through-ninth-place winners, Gayle received a trophy.

*Gayle Kermode with the trophy she received for being sixth-place winner in the 1978 All-American Soap Box Derby.*

*Gayle Kermode, sixth-place winner in the 1978 All-American Soap Box Derby where she represented Los Angeles County. When she returned home from Akron, the local newspaper interviewed her.*

The Junior Division winners received power tools. Special awards were given for best constructed car, best interior, most original design, and fastest time in a heat. In addition, all the champions received other mementos: racing helmets, jackets, cameras, tennis shoes, T-shirts, skateboards, and tennis balls.

The most moving event of the evening was when the parents of the 169 local champions gave their youngsters a standing ovation. They were still champions!

Gayle had recovered her usual good spirits by the time she left for home. "I had the *best* time this week," she giggled. "It was fun meeting new kids from all over the country!" Then, a little sad: "I *am* sorry I can't race at Akron any more." Her mood picked up again as she remembered: "Oh, well, I can still race in the rallies."

And she has continued to do just that, winning regularly in local rallies in Southern California. If her love of racing continues, she might just wind up at Indianapolis someday!

# Index

Italics indicate illustration.

# About the Author

Sylvia A. Rosenthal grew up in East Orange, New Jersey. After a year of college in Phoenix, Arizona, she moved to Southern California, where she worked for many top screenwriters and was told that she should take up writing. Instead, she married and had a family. When her two daughters were eight and eleven, she returned to college and then spent twenty years as an elementary school teacher in Los Angeles. Now she is writing, taking journalism courses, and has taught creative writing to fourth- and fifth-graders at the Burbank, California, library.

Her enthusiasm for soap box derby racing was kindled when Burbank, for the first time in twenty years, held a local race. "I started attending the workshops and practice runs," Mrs. Rosenthal says. "I loved mingling with the children and liked the spirit behind the whole thing. It is fun, exciting, but not win-at-any-cost. This is one sport that almost anyone can engage in."